THIS IS HOW I KEEP YOU

KRISTINA MAHR

"The center of every poem is this:
I have loved you.
I have had to deal with that."

- Salma Deera -

OTHER POETRY COLLECTIONS
BY KRISTINA MAHR

Keep a Weather Eye

I escort visitors around this break like
it's a crack in the foundation. I say, *keep a*
weather eye, it's dark down there. I say,
watch where you're stepping, it's deep
down there. I try to warn them but they
still fall in, and I can't pull them back
out. (Can I?) I watch them pull themselves
free. I watch them go with sad eyes like
I'm not holding the door open for them,
like my hand's not on the small of their
backs, pushing.

They leave covered in cuts and breaks and
I send them home with apologies to staunch
the bleeding.

Does it do any good?

I close the door
                    before I ever know.

The One Who Wields It

Whatever has kept you
can keep you.

I have befriended the silence
and now I'm the one
who wields it.

Survivor

With you standing beside me,
I knew I could survive anything.

Now I know it because
I survived losing you.

Nothing but Ghosts

In a dream I fly out west and knock on your
door and nobody answers. I ask the neighbor
if she's seen you and she says, *honey, that*
house has been empty for years, she says,
honey, the only ones living there
have been ghosts.

Ghosts, nothing but ghosts. Ghosts laughing,
ghosts dancing. Ghosts saying it's love, ghosts
saying it's not. Ghosts leaving, ghosts pleading,
ghosts on the floor bleeding.

In a dream you were never real and
neither were we.

Of all the goddamn dreams why
was this the one that had to
come true.

What Love Is

I used to say
if that's not love
then I don't know what
love is.

It turns out
I don't know what
love is.

Shot in the Dark

We were a shot in the dark but when the lights
came on the walls were bloody and you were
gone. I guess we missed. I guess I missed. I
guess I am the one missing.

Three billion years from now the Milky Way will
collide with the Andromeda Galaxy and
astronomers say it will be chaos. (I mean three
billion years from when I loved you.) (I mean
three billion years and seven months from when
you loved me.) There will be stars crashing into one
another, orbits thrown out of whack. Just between
us I'm sad to miss it. Once the chaos ends, they will
be one big galaxy and I bet it will be beautiful. I
mean, whatever's left of it.

God tell me how you're the one gone
and I am the one

        missing.

And Now I Can't

I couldn't
make you
love me,

and now
I can't
let him.

What Am I But

What am I but heartbroken. But aching, but
drowning, but wanting. What am I but what
you left. But what you did not ache for, drown
for, want.

What am I but not enough to keep you.

At the corner of the chalkboard in my kitchen
is a smudge where I erased the countdown I
used to keep of how many days until I'd get
to see you.

I don't know how to count down to never.

You can lead a horse to water, but
you can't make it drink.

I can tell you that I love you, but
I can't make you stay.

The Thing We Could Have Been

I mind less that you broke
the thing we were
and more that you broke
the thing we could have been.

Where You Were

Say what you want about running from your
past, but in my experience it's easier than
running back to it. In my experience the past
is a sidewalk dropping away behind me as
the present drags me forward. I turn around
and it's gone. I turn around and I'm not sure
it was ever there.

Some days I want to fall away with it.

I want to let it take me where you went.

I want to live where you are.

Where you were, I mean.

Where you were and
where I was when
you and I were

us.

I Do

When they walk away
shaking their heads and
saying I just don't know
what I want, I want to
shout after them that
the trouble is, I do.

It just doesn't want me back.

This Is How I Keep You

Things don't hurt you the same way they hurt me.

I can count on one hand the number of times I heard
you say my name, while yours was and ever has been
every word but amen in every one of my prayers.

This is how I keep you —

tucked between my clasped fingers
    beneath my bowed head.

This is how I keep you —

locked inside a forgiveness
    I can't give you if you're not sorry.

If you don't open the box, the cat is both
alive and dead.

If I don't ever talk to you again, you both
still love me and you don't.

This is how I keep you —

like the loudest silence.

Like the quietest
                    scream.

When I Let It

I'm starting to think
that the answer to
when does this pain end

is

    when

        I

          let it.

Categories of Gone

I look in your eyes now and see suns setting
instead of rising and I know there will be late
fees on this time. I know it's overdue. I know
we have crossed somehow from almost to
already in the categories of gone, and I wonder
when it happened. How I missed the moment.
Why I couldn't stop it. We fell out like a fraying
rope; there was no severing. No cleaving. Only
wearing, only wearying, only the sea and the
storms and the way you stopped sending me
good morning texts. Only the way I stopped
expecting them.

I close my eyes so I can't see you go, but
you go in ways I can't miss.

Your hand in my rib cage.

Your voice in my ear.

You go in ways that years from now
I know I won't
                    stop missing.

The Cracks Inside of It

Sometimes I'm a body and sometimes I'm the girl
inside of it. Sometimes I'm the heart inside of her.
Sometimes I'm the cracks inside of it.

Einstein said either everything's a miracle or
nothing is but that means if you and me were a
miracle then somehow you leaving has to be too.

My neighbor sits in his parked car in his driveway
every day and listens to old love songs, and I wonder
if he can't bring himself to go inside because it's
empty or because it isn't.

Is he the one with cracks inside his heart or is he
the one making them.

I love you. I still say your name sometimes. I finally
believe you're never coming back. I finally believe

     I don't want you to.

More Than This

There is always going to be more than this,
even on the days
you're sure there has never
been less than this.

It's a Long Story

When people ask about us I say it's a long story like I
don't want to tell it but I do. I want to tell them how
we met and I want to tell them how you left.

I want to tell them every time our paths cross I love
you a little harder and you hurt me a little deeper.

I want to tell them I almost called you last night but
didn't because if it's hell not hearing your voice it's a
different kind of hell hearing it tell me goodbye.

I want to tell them I think I'll spend my whole life
wondering if you meant anything you said to me and
if you ever wish you hadn't said it or if you ever
wish you could've kept it.

I want to tell them about the first night, and I want to
tell them about the last night, and I want to tell them
I loved you. I want to tell them you loved me.

It's what I want to tell them.

Not what I can.

Braver

I can't say for sure that
anything you might have said
would have been better than
this silence, but

I can say for sure that
it would have
been braver.

The Past Tense of Losing

It is hard to let anybody love me ever since
you didn't. I don't know how to do this. I'm
sorry to say that sometimes this still breaks
me. Some days, some nights. I have brittle
not loving you bones and they can't always
hold all the weight of this. How heavy is
absence. How filled with emptiness. How
staggering this still.

Lost is the past tense of losing, but it isn't
always, right? Tell me it isn't always. Tell
me sometimes the things you lose

are how you're someday found.

I Don't Deserve This

I still think the thought

I don't deserve this.

It just means the opposite
of what it used to.

Something Sweet

I stick it to the bathroom
mirror. Tuck it
into your sock drawer. Slip it
into the back
pocket of your favorite jeans
(—my
favorite jeans.) Clip it to your
driver
side visor. Leave it in a
voicemail. Whisper
it against your heartbeat. Trail
it across
your chest. Rewrite it as
promises.
Translate it into sighs.

Write something sweet, they tell
me.

They don't know that when I
do
I write it just for you.

This Willful Thing

I understand that I will not love you anymore is
different than I do not love you anymore is
different than I cannot love you anymore. I have
seen enough toddlers stomp their feet and cross
their arms to know what this is. This willful
thing. This unyielding thing. I have been on the
receiving end of enough I can'ts to know when
they're really I won'ts.

I will not love you anymore.

I am stomping my feet—
                              (do you hear me.)

I am crossing my arms—
                              (do you see me.)

I will not love you anymore.

   (I can't.)

Time

Time's been tugging you free of me and I've started
to think, *you can have him.* You heal all wounds? Heal
his wounds. That boy's got wounds so deep I never
did reach the bottom of them, though I tried, I tried,
no one can say I didn't try, he can't say I didn't try.
All that love I poured inside of them and I never
heard it hit the bottom, never saw it reach the surface,
never heard it echo.

Time's been ripping you free of me and
I've been thinking about your hands.

I've been thinking about your voice.

I've been thinking about the morning you woke to me
too far away and pulled me bodily
across the bed and into you.

I've been thinking about what I'd keep
if I had a say in it.

I open my mouth to speak but—

    time may heal all wounds but
    it also waits for no one.

(It didn't wait for me.)

All the Things You Can Do

I am never anything less than amazed
by all the things you can do.

I just wish one of them was love me.

The Worst Thing

God I hope this is
the worst thing you ever did
to somebody who loved you.

You Leaving in My Eye

I'm not crying, that's just dust, that's just the
sun, that's just you leaving in my eye. Tell me
how we survive this. Not you and me but you.
and me.

My heart keeps insisting we ran out of pages
before we ran out of story so I give us endings
we didn't have, which is to say, I give us one.

No one tells you that sometimes heaven
comes at a price and that price
                                  is
                                        hell.

Teeth Marks

I hold swatches up against your cruelty but
I can't match it. The closest I've come is I
didn't wish you a happy birthday this year
and there are teeth marks on my insides
from where it ate at me. So tell me — are
you shredded beneath your skin. Is your
heart crumbs. Are your lungs scraps.
Honey, are the vultures circling, have they
picked your bones clean. Honey, what's left
of you. Honey, what hasn't left of you.

I have stayed so quiet. so quiet.

But I can't hear you when you don't speak.

Walkie-Talkie

The first time I used a walkie-talkie I didn't realize
holding the button down to speak meant I
couldn't hear what was being said.

How much do we miss
every time we aren't quiet.

So I stay quiet but I

still miss you.

The Gift That Keeps on Giving

Pain doesn't wrap neatly so you put it in a gift
bag. You write love before your name on the
tag but if you really loved me I wonder if
you'd be giving me this. You shove tissue
paper softness down on top of it but making it
pretty doesn't make it weigh any less, doesn't
make it hurt any less. I say thank you when
you give it to me but you say *don't thank me yet.*
God don't thank me yet.

I know you got it from her. I wonder who she
got it from.

It's the gift that keeps on giving but
I wish you could
stop giving it.

Are You Ready?

I have sharpened my words to a point but instead of driving it home I circle the block three times and let the songs on the radio tell you all the things I'm too afraid to. This ends tonight but how remains to be seen. Fire or its absence. Fire or its absence. The only way to kill certain types of fire is to remove all the oxygen and I guess that's what type of fire we are because we're dying and I can't breathe.

And none of this looked a thing like poetry until I wrestled it onto this paper and ironed it flat but now it's capable of shallow cuts, now I don't have to worry about losing blood just by holding it too close.

Now I can put it somewhere you can read it when you're ready instead of howling it to the sky.

Are you ready?

I wouldn't have said this last night and I doubt
I will tomorrow, but if you called me tonight
I would answer.

Secrets

I keep your secrets
though I've become
one of them.

The First Time

Maya Angelou said, "When someone
shows you who they are believe them
the first time," but I didn't.

I didn't believe you the first time.

I didn't believe you the second time.

But I
      believe
            you now.

Hey Taylor

Hey Taylor,

I think he knows. That this is the last time, that we can't begin again, that everything has changed. I tell him, *you can call it what you want but that won't change what it is.* (Treacherous.) (Haunted.) He tells me, *you need to calm down.* He tells me, *you belong with me.*

Hey Taylor,

I wish you would tell me why I can't shake it off. Why the very first night I had to fight the urge to run. Why he's just on the other side of the door but I can't bring myself to breathe, let alone speak now.

Hey Taylor,

You said 'tis the damn season but I guess you didn't mean for a love story. I know all too well it's time to go so don't blame me if I almost do.

This is me trying not to.

My Muse

You are not my muse.

Your absence is.

Honey

Honey I fought for this, got lost
for this, saw most of my heart
broken off for this, honey I tried
for this, truth be told lied for this,
late at night quietly cried for this,
honey I believed in this, begged
on my knees for this, hugged my
own waist as I grieved for this,
honey, honey, honey, I can't

do this anymore. Can't wait by
the phone anymore. Can't wish
you'd be someone you're not
anymore. Can't wish you'd be
someone

you never were

anymore.

Chasing You

The only reason I spent so long
chasing you is because that's
what I heard you're supposed to
do with dreams.

With Me

I want you to be happy but
not as much as I wanted
you to be happy
with me.

With Love

I let you go with love.

(With what little you left me.)

Burned

The thing about rising
from the ashes is that
now your wings are fire and
everything you touch
comes away

burned.

My Comfort Heartbreak

Baby that's my comfort
heartbreak, it bleeds me
lullabies, I can't sleep
without its screams.
I spent years grabbing
love's lapels and begging
it not to go and now I hang
from heartbreak's hem and
kindly ask it for the same.
Don't leave me. Don't leave
me why does everybody leave
me. leave me. leave me.

I am trying to convince
the stars to shine
in a sky without
you in it.

Rock the Boat

They say don't rock the boat but how else
am I supposed to slosh all this water out
over the sides. It's up to our necks in here,
up to our chins, up to our noses, we're
drowning in here, don't you want us to stop
drowning in here. I've been bailing us out
for months, quietly, cupped hands, keeping
this boat still, but it filled faster than I
could bail it.

So now I rock the boat.

If you fall out with the water
maybe you were never meant
to be in here with me
in the first place.

Snowbird

You snowbird in my
mind, still. Long winter
months, it's warm in
here, you stay.

Come summer I'll be busy,
you'll be elsewhere, but
for now I dream
your name.

The Lions of Tsavo

I stuff my heart like the man-eating lions in the
Field Museum — jaw open, mid-roar. (Did they
really do all the things they said they did; did they
mean to?) Stick it in a glass case rigged with
alarms and a superfluous sign that says *Don't
Touch*. Look closely you can see that it is held
together by pins. Look closely you can see
all the places where it broke.

Men with nice smiles buy replicas from the
souvenir shop and can't even tell
the difference.

Can't even tell
they don't beat.

Can't even tell
you're not in there.

Can't even tell
I'm not either.

You Coward

I've been checking obituaries
again. Reading off names,
thinking about how every loss
is someone's. Wondering if
your loss will still be mine, all
these years later. Wondering if
anything short of seeing
your name on these pages
would make this feel
done, would let me move on.

I still loved you on the nights
you wouldn't let me call it that.

Call me, you
               coward.

Closer

We looked at the same love but it
was like an embroidery hoop where
I only saw the beauty of us and you
only saw the tangled mess.

Neither of us can say we
truly saw it for what it was, but
I still think I
came closer.

Let Go

You may have moved on but
you took me with you.

You were supposed to tell me
to let go first.

(You were supposed to let go first.)

Your City

People vacation in your city, and when they ask if I've
been, I say if you have some time to kill you should
spend an hour wandering around Bay Books;
sometimes they give you a free pin which will end up
in a box in your closet with his name on it, and who
knows, you might keep it forever, you might never be
able to bring yourself to throw it away. I say the views
from the Fortuna trails are to die for, if you aren't too
scared of winding roads and scrambling hikes and
him not looking at you. I say you might get
sunburned, though, and you might still carry those tan
lines many months later, long after he says he doesn't
love you anymore. I say the airport is so easy to
navigate, and no one bats an eye if you sob what's left
of your heart out at your gate.

People vacation in your city, and when
they ask if I've been, I say part of me
    never
        left.

What I Choose to Keep of Us

We are now what I choose to keep
of us. What I see from where I sit,
based on the angle I set us down.
The degree to which I open the
blinds to let the light shine on us.
How carefully I place us. How
empty I keep the space beside us.

We are now as much as I can bear.

I forget the rest of us.

I bear the best of us.

How Beautifully

Look at all that I have built upon
the mouth of our grave.

If we ever claw our way free,
all of this would crumble.

But I can't help thinking
how beautifully we
could rebuild it
together.

Even If

I don't love the things
that hurt me anymore.

Even if they say
it'll be different this time.

Unheard

California breaks my heart. I step off the
plane and the earth quakes but nobody else
seems to feel it. No I'm sorry that's just the
tired talking, that's just the retrograde
talking, that's just the holes inside of me I
keep falling in talking. I don't miss you if I
don't think of you but California makes me
think of you, just like ferries do, just like
starry skies do, just like most days and most
nights do. That doesn't mean it's still love,
just that I'm still littered with what ifs.

I take solace in the fact
that I left nothing unsaid
regardless that you left it all

unheard.

Closure

The only closure I need
is the kind where this door
stays closed.

The Sea I Cried

When my heart broke, half of it fell into the sea. The sea I cried? The sea. I thought it might float but it sank to the bottom. Became a hollow home to anemones and *answer me*s. From the half that was left, I slid a sliver of it beneath your fingernail so everything new you touched would hurt and make you think of me. You flinched and tried to claw it free but you didn't, did you. You couldn't, could you. One shard is in my throat so that every goodbye I say drips with blood. Another piece I turn to crumbs and I drop them wherever I go. *Follow them.* There is a shred of it stuck between my teeth that tastes of you. There is a scrap of it like a rock in my shoe that makes every step forward hurt.

There is a small bit of it still beating in my chest. Still beating. Still beating.

And in these words I bury
what needs burying.

At the End

It is human nature, at the end, to think of
the beginning. To wonder how we got
from there to here. To hug something
gone cold and remember it warm. To
mourn it, to grieve it, to fall to your knees
beneath it. To refuse to believe it.

I always knew one day I would
kiss you for the last time but
I didn't know it'd be
this morning.

Can't Stop

You can't stop me
from loving you
any more than
I can stop you
from leaving me.

Space

When I say I need space I mean place me
among the stars. I mean let me lie in the
curve of the moon. I mean I am learning
to dodge asteroids. I mean I am trying to
tame comets.

When I say I need space I mean I am tired
of letting gravity hold me down.

And I mean I will still love you
when I come back down to earth.

No, I mean I will love you

better.

Bury Me

I scream wrecking balls into
your wall of silence.

But when it crumbles,
all it does
is bury me.

If You Weren't Sure

I have taken tests before where
if you don't know the answer you
shouldn't guess, because
leaving it blank is better
than getting it wrong.

Which is to say, if you
weren't sure you loved
me, you just shouldn't
have said anything.

It would've hurt less
than you realizing
you got it wrong.

Valentine

I cut so carefully along the lines
of this valentine but the scissors slip
and the heart I give you is jagged-edged
and less than whole.

Honey, the only love I've ever been sold I bought
in an alley some September, and it looked so pretty
I paid full price before I even checked to see if it was
real. I spent eight months watching it slip through my
fingers like ashes but instead of sprinkling them on
ice so I wouldn't slip walking home I gathered them
up to see if they could somehow spark a flame.

Needless to say they couldn't and I
slipped and I never made it home.

This is all to say I made you a valentine.

I know I said it wasn't whole
but it's my whole broken heart.

Let It

I don't stand by with a fire extinguisher
anymore anytime someone tells me
they love me.

If it wants to burn down,
I'm going to
let it.

Flattened Faster

They say it is better to be
on the right hand of the devil than
in his path, but I have had to be both
over the course of loving you, and
I can tell you with certainty —

when you're by his side, you can't
get a clear look at his face
to know if he's lying
when he tells you that
he loves you.

When you're in his path, at least,
you're flattened
faster.

Dancing with My Demons

He asks me to dance but I say honey my dance
card is full, I'm dancing with my demons tonight.
That one dances slow, real slow, slow like time,
slow like healing, and that one dances fast, real
fast, fast like it's over, fast like you're gone. Some
of them spin me dizzy, some of them two-step in
time with the ringing in my ears, with the
streaming of my tears. At last call they all come
home with me, I'm that kind of girl now, did you
know I'm that kind of girl now.

There's room
for all of us
in my bed
now that you
and love
aren't in it.

For Breaking

I'm sorry that someone
made you think
that hearts were made
for breaking.

What Comes After

I am not afraid
of love, I am
afraid of what
comes after.

By My Fingertips

Still now years later when I draw love
I draw myself dangling by my fingertips
from the edge of a cliff.

I never know where to draw you, though.

Were you standing at the top,
could you have pulled me up?

Or were you standing at the bottom,
could you have caught me?

I guess it doesn't matter
what you *could* have done.

Young Love

I drive past the spot and we are
still there. Young love. A beginning.
You have never seen me cry and I
have never heard you mad. A drunk
girl passes by and you wrap your arms
around me. The moon is out. Or it isn't.
I can't remember, I can't see it, all I see
is us. The bar is closed, the girl
is gone, and it's just us.

I drive past the spot and I don't
stop. I swallow every warning
my heart begs me to scream.

It is broken now but
as I watch our first kiss
I know someday
it will be glad I let us have this.

A Goddamn Shame

He hands me flowers that died when we
did and waits for me to resurrect them.
Blames me for giving up when I bury
what he killed. Blames me for walking
out of a room he set on fire. Blames me
for thriving when the most either of us
thought I could hope for was surviving.

Blames me for not still calling
two years after he stopped answering.

We might be
a goddamn shame
but I'm not the one
who shamed us.

Like Snow in March

You love me like snow in
March — unexpectedly.
infrequently. just as I
start to get reaccustomed
to warmth. just as I throw
open all of my windows.
just as I start to dream
of summer.

You love me like snow in
March.

And you're gone
just as
quickly.

For Anything

I won't ask you for anything
you can't give anymore.

An explanation, an apology.

Kindness, your heart.

I won't ask you for anything
you don't have anymore.

This Paper Pavement

Love? No—scared boy like a pebble my heart
tripped over, skinning both its knees and spilling
poems like blood all over this paper pavement.
Drip drip dripping so many words I could tie them
end to end and almost reach where you are if you
were somewhere I could reach. Scared boy. Pebble
boy. Strip strip stripping love like paint from my
bones with every minute you aren't brave. Aren't
trying. Aren't here. Scared boy. Pebble boy. Love-
stripped boy. What else. What else. Grip grip
gripping. (Me.) Trip trip tripping. (Me.) What else.

A story I tell that never ends well.

Not a love story. Not a love story.

A poem I keep writing
even though I know
how it ends.

You Don't Get To

I keep thinking the thought *you don't
get to*, like you don't get to walk away
like that, like you don't get to treat me
like that, like you don't get to pretend
you're doing this for me like that.

It works both ways though.

You don't get to be forgiven for that.

You don't get to ever again be
somebody I'm in love with
after that.

Was There a Moment

Is your heart not broken? Did
losing me not chip it, dent it,
crack it? Come on, bruise it,
leave the tiniest of marks on it?
I'm not asking did it scar it. I'm
not asking did it ruin it. I'm
asking was there a moment

when it bled.

I'm asking was there a moment
when losing me

hurt.

Lost Without You

When I say I am lost without you I mean
I am something small inside my heart
trying to find my way through
the cracks in it.

No Hard Feelings

You read somewhere
that if you make
a fist, that's the
approximate size of
your heart, so you
make a fist but
all it ever does
is the wrong kind
of beating.

The kind that leaves
it empty when you
open it.

I say no hard feelings, but
that doesn't mean
there are any
soft ones.

Five Years Ago Today

Snapchat asks me if I remember what I was doing five
years ago today and goddammit I was trying not to, all
I'm ever doing is trying not to. I know I was sitting
on the floor of a house I don't go to anymore, calling
a dog who isn't alive anymore, in love with a man I
don't know anymore. I look at the photos anyway. I
watch the video. I watch that dog run toward me,
tripping over her feet, all joy. All glee. She puts my
whole hand in her mouth and I say, *gentle. Gentle.*

Five years from now if Snapchat asks me
if I remember what I was doing five years
ago — today — I'll know

my whole heart was in my mouth
and blood was dripping down my throat
and god none of this
was gentle.

Who Will

If you don't love me anymore, who will tell me
to look at the moon. Who will I tell to look at
the moon. Who will whisper constellations
into my skin, who will I name hurricanes after.
Who will we tell stories to, or of, or for. Beneath
or between or upon. Who will see I'm trying, god,
I'm trying, who will believe me, who will believe
in me. Who will I believe in. Who will catch me
when I fall or run or look away, who will I be
looking for. Or at. Or through.

If you don't love me anymore, who will I call when I
have a bad dream. Who will I call when that bad
dream's that you don't love me anymore.

If you don't love me anymore—

                                    who will.

Things We Didn't Mean

In the end,
we both said things
we didn't mean.

I said
I never wanted to see you again.

You said
you'd always love me.

If Love Forgets

If love forgets then why do I remember.

I watch doorways and thresholds and corners and
remember a time when you'd pass through them and
over them and around them and your eyes would
scan the crowd and I would always know
you were looking for me.

Absence taps me on the shoulder and
reminds me it's still here.

I know.
I know.

I betrayed my body
in the same way I betrayed
my heart—

I let

you touch it.

The Place I Live

Nowadays I paint myself in
my favorite colors instead
of yours.

When I finally come home
to myself, I want to like
the place
I live.

You Told the World You Did

Did he break your heart, too. Did he love you, really
love you, say he really loved you, and then leave you.
Leave you questioning if he loved you, really loved
you. Did you keep fighting for him, keep losing pieces
of yourself for him, spend years searching for
everything you lost for him.

Did he come back and say he loved you again.

Did you try again.

Did he break you again, make you crazy again, did
you leave him, did *you* leave *him*, did you do
everything you could 'til you knew
this time you had to fight for you.

I assume you did, you told the world you did

when you stole the words I wrote
that told the world

I did.

Your Sweet Heart

Tell me does your heart still beat. beat. beat around
the bush, pretending there are *I love you* petals mixed
in with the *I love you not* petals you rip from me before
claiming I'm all thorns. Tell me do you feel your heart
break. break. break mine every minute you don't call
my bluff and lay every card you've held close to your
chest on the table between us.

Every card you've held close to your beat. beat.
beating heart as you break. break. break mine.

Tell me, sweetheart,

is there any part of your sweet heart

that wishes you hadn't

wrecked me.

Staying

For some people, leaving
is the hardest thing
in the world.

For other people, it's

staying.

Cloud Nine

You can survive a fall from cloud one. Let's say,
you see him across the bar at closing time and he
smiles — if you never see him again you'll survive
it. Cloud two's a little higher (let's say he asks for
your number) but has nothing on cloud three (let's
say that's your first date.) The air is thinner on
cloud four, when he kisses you for the first time.
Cloud five clouds the senses (date two, no, date
three,) cloud six you're high enough to see above
the trees (a week has passed, now two, now three.)
Cloud seven has you dodging airplanes (god that
night, that one, that one.) Cloud eight? Cloud
eight, it's cold up here, but his arms keep you
warm. On cloud nine he says he loves you, but I
want to make it clear —

you won't survive
the fall from here.

Why Aren't You

I have reached for stars in the sky
less out of reach than you.

I tell myself it is better to be
the aftermath than the war but it is
too quiet here; not enough hearts
are beating here; everyone can hear me
screaming here.

The calendar said last week was spring
but now the flowers say it too.

The geese are flying home
so why aren't you.

If You Tell a Poet You Love Her

If you tell a poet you love
her, she'll turn you into
poetry. If she turns you
into poetry, she might find
a way to keep you. If she
finds a way to keep you,
she might wish someday
she hadn't. If she wishes
someday she hadn't, she
might have a broken heart.
If she has a broken heart,
she might turn it into poetry.

And if she turns it into
poetry, she might be able
to bear it.

Not Everything

Alone is a new house I am just beginning to
make a home. I chop the wood, I light the
match, I sit in front of the fire. I keep it
burning. I keep myself warm.

If I never hear from you again, I will believe
the best of you. I will believe the worst of you.
I will believe nothing but the best or worst of
you—there is no grey in your gone.

I've been here so long I've forgotten
how to be anywhere else.

Not everything is meant to be ours

(—but god some of it could've been.)

Show, Don't Tell

Do not tell me your heart is broken; show me
its pieces. Show me your tear-stained
pillowcase. Show me your tear-pooled eyes.
Show me your shaking hands, your clenched
jaw. Show me the hole missing me punched in
your bedroom wall. Show me the words
needing me howled in your sleep. Show me
the bruises kneeling left on your knees from
pleading my forgiveness.

Do not tell me your heart is broken.

I can't keep pretending
it's you and me at the end of this
when it's only been me
through every
hurt of this.

Masquerade

Our love was a masquerade; you
wore a mask, and I thought
I'd recognize you
without it.

No Rhyme or Reason

I have not touched you in years so I wrote you
into this poem; it's the only way I still know how
to feel you. Honey you feel like everything I
never got the chance to say. Honey you feel like
the space between the last time I heard your
voice and forever. The haunting of unrequited
wanting. A rending of an ending.

Someone told me it's not poetry unless
it rhymes or unless
there's a reason for it.

But I loved you without rhyme.

I loved you without
                                        reason.

Unburdened

Unburdened of my love and trust,

tell me —

do you feel

free

enough.

Come to Your Senses

I won't lie to you, I don't wish you well. I
wish the taste of me on your tongue. I wish
the sound of my laugh in your ears. I wish
the scent of my skin in your nose. I wish
the sight of my wanting you in your eyes
every time you close them.

I wish the feel of me in your arms. On
your fingertips. Across your body.

I don't wish you well, I wish you
would come to my senses.

If you did, you'd find me
in all of them.

No One Else

Do you ever think of the things you broke me for?
How many nights, how few mornings. To feel
wanted, perhaps? To feel for a little while like you
weren't alone before you made me feel the most
alone I've ever felt, perhaps? Did you enjoy
watching me fight tooth and nail for what you
knew you would not want for long. When I called
and told you I was broken did you think that it was
worth it. Did it seem worth it. Did you love me
hard enough for it to have been worth it.

I have drowned in you leaving and I have
drowned in you staying. Drowning is
drowning, but at least when you left, I knew —

no one else was going to save me.

Incomplete

I am not a
complete mess
without you; I am
an incomplete one.

Still and Only Ever

This is not the part where you come back. This is
not the part where you explain why you left, or
how you left, or god how could you leave, this is
not the part where I understand how you could
leave. If this is the part where you realize you were
wrong, that's one thing, but this is not the part
where you tell me. This is not the part where I
forgive you, nor is this the part where you ask it of
me. (This could be the part where I forgive you if
you would just ask it of me.)

This is not the part where I forget you. This is not
the part where I say definitively that I no
longer love you.

This is still and only ever
the part where I'm
without you.

Thursday's Child

Thursday's child has far to go

but fights tooth and nail to get there. Doesn't stop.
Hasn't stopped. Has far to go but has come so far.
Believes. Believes. Believes in the journey as well as
the destination. Knows. Doesn't just think, hope,
want but *knows* where she wants to go, how she
wants to get there, that she *can* get there.

Thursday's child's heart is broken. Has been
broken. Will be broken again.

But Thursday's child is halfway up a mountain
she'll never be back at the bottom of.

She may have far to go but she'll
have a hell of a view
as she gets there.

Different Than This

Hide my pen. Stop letting me bleed all over
what too many trees have died for. Stop letting
me carve myself hollow like the right words in
the right order might bring him back. I want
less than this. I want more than this.

Next time I fall it won't be into
arms that cannot hold me or for
men who cannot catch me. It
won't be for pretty words or
faces or lies.

I want
different
than this.

Never Even Close

There are too many
city lights out here
to see the stars, but
I paint them on my
bedroom ceiling,
and I look at pictures,
and I tell myself it's
almost the same.

I passed a picture of you
in my phone yesterday.

You know, I don't need
to see real stars to know —

it has never
been even close to
the same.

Wasted

As for us, we were
drunk on love, wasted
on love, no —

love
was wasted
on us.

The Message

Your silence makes a
poor secretary. I tell it
I miss you but

you never
get
the message.

Where I Touch
after Mark Strand

Where I touch,
the sky cannot.

When I lean
into you, my forehead
pressed up into
yours, my arms around
your waist, the sky folds
in around us.

We all have reasons
to walk away.

I walk away
so the sky can
reach you.

*I walk away so you
can reach the sky.*

Infinite

If there's a version of you that never
left me, there must also be a version
of you that never loved me. A version
of me that never met you. A version of
me that saw it coming when you left
me. A version of the bar where we met
that closed early that night. A version of
that last flight that was canceled. A version
of this poem that ends in some way other than—

if there are infinite versions
of infinite moments, and
every possibility exists
in some place, in some time—

there must be a version of my heart
that is no longer broken
because the version of you that loved me
became the version of you that
left me.

You Can

Honey you can cry on my shoulder just
be careful of my sleeve, I keep my heart
there. I mean be careful if you don't
want it. I mean it's yours if you want it.

If you think you can hurt me—

you're right, you can.

I guess I don't understand
why you'd want to.

Blood and Broken

If love is everything what is all the rest of this.

My heart pumps blood and love for you
through my veins and I think I need a
transfusion; I can't have loving you in
my legs (I will walk to you.) I can't have
loving you in my arms (I will reach for you.)

My heart pumps blood and broken through
my veins and this is fine. this is fine. this is fine.

Instead of a to-do list I write down
every promise you ever made me but
there is nothing satisfying
about crossing them off
one

by

one.

It All

Winner takes it all but there are no winners
here, no one to claim it all, who gets it all, not
us. We left it all in the gutter on some city
streets somewhere past midnight and in the
morning neither of us could remember where
we left it.

Somewhere we could see the stars.

Somewhere you said things and I felt things.

Somewhere we knew what it all was for
before we let it all go
to waste.

Some of It

I have never loved
myself less than when
I loved you.

And while most of
that's on me—

some of it's on
you, too.

I Want to Tell You

I want to tell you you'll be fine.

I want to tell you I've been there and
it was misery and agony and I know
you'll be fine because one day I was fine.

The next day I wasn't again.

I wasn't again.

I wasn't again.

But I want to tell you the day came again
when I was fine. And yes, okay, the next
day I wasn't again, but I was a little less
not fine that day. And a little more fine
when I was fine again.

And a little less, and a little more,
and so it went, and so it goes.

I want to tell you you'll be fine.

But I also want to tell you
it's okay to still be sad.

A Reckoning

Each poem is a reckoning; a firing squad I stand
before, heart in hand, praying for a pardon. I have
done these things. There, a confession, in writing—
I have done these things. Loved? Yes. Lost? *Yes.*
Loved still?

…

I have done these things.

I will not face the wall.

I will not close my eyes to what
has closed its eyes to me.

There is a world in which I live for
the things that I am dying for.

There is a world in which the heart I hold
still belongs to me.

I have done these things.

I do not take any of this lightly.

Both Pieces

My heart may be in two, but
both pieces belong
to you.

The Silence

We never break the silence, we just set it aside.

You are so gentle with it, so
delicate. You love it, I think. As much
as you can love anything, you love
this silence, you nurture it, you let it
speak for you.

And I have tried to shatter it, but
I cannot even dent it. You have fed it
too well, built it too strong.

Loved it too dearly.

It makes me think
how strong I might have been
if you had loved me,
too.

Too Clean

Bones break, hearts don't.

Hearts give out (they can't keep doing
this.) Hearts murmur (and we don't
listen.) Hearts skip beats (and we'll
never get those back.)

Hearts are a muscle and
muscles don't break.

Muscles tear.

Muscles rip.

Muscles rupture.

I just want to be clear because
a break sounds too clean

for what this was.

A Name

I gave love
a name it doesn't answer to,
and now it won't come back.

(I gave it yours.)

CONTENTS

ACKNOWLEDGMENTS

I am writing these acknowledgments on the five year anniversary of the breakup that started it all, back when I thought of it as the breakup that ended it all.

So I acknowledge the magical healing powers of time & words.

I acknowledge the knee-deep gratitude I feel to be sitting where I am, surrounded by who I am.

And I acknowledge that whatever or whomever the catalyst was, I created all of this.

And I will never not be proud of it.

ABOUT THE AUTHOR

Kristina Mahr devotes her days to real people and her nights to fictional ones. She works full-time in employee relations in the suburbs of Chicago, but her true passion is writing. In her spare time, she enjoys spending time with her family, friends, and small herd of rescue animals, as well as waking up at the crack of dawn every weekend to watch the Premier League.

You can find more information about her other poetry collections, as well as her fiction novels on her website at:

www.kristinamahr.com

83471807R00075